T0105552

Order this book online at www.trafford.com
or email orders@trafford.com

Most Trafford titles are also available at major online book retailers.

Printed in the United States of America.

ISBN: 978-1-4269-3808-5 (sc)
ISBN: 978-1-4269-3810-8 (e-book)

Library of Congress Control Number: 2010910595

*Our mission is to efficiently provide the world's finest, most comprehensive book publishing
service, enabling every author to experience success. To find out how to publish your book,
your way, and have it available worldwide, visit us online at www.trafford.com*

Trafford rev. 7/23/2010

 www.trafford.com

North America & international
toll-free: 1 888 232 4444 (USA & Canada)
phone: 250 383 6864 ♦ fax: 812 355 4082

DEDICATION

For my dad, who left this world way too soon but stayed long enough
to teach me the gift of talking and building relationships with others.
For my wife Holly who has always given me enough
space to act on my dreams and my three kids, Nicolai,
Scout, and Cross who gave me the reason to write this book
and all the other things I do to make their lives better.
For the Walden's; Bobby and Scarlett, for without them,
none of this would have even been a dream much less a reality

EPIGRAPH

"Helping somebody is what it is all about; that is what I enjoy doing"-
Bobby Walden

"The reason I helped you is because I could; that means

I am obliged to help you"- Joe Gilliam

FOREWORD

Peter,

It doesn't seem like that long ago - but it has been a few years since we sneaked you on the team bus and into the game. It was a bit risky but fun ushering you on with the team, explaining to the bus driver you were family. Your friends had tickets and we couldn't let you miss the game. You know Peter fans like you are one of the main reasons I enjoyed playing football. We were there to celebrate and have fun. Getting you in and past security made it more fun for everybody. We are all a bunch of big kids.

Good luck with your book!!

Sincerely,
Bobby Walden
39
Pittsburgh Steelers

PREFACE

The reasons I wrote this book are many, however, most importantly, I wanted to show the world that a regular guy can make substantial headway by fostering relationships with good people. I once listened to John Brady, former head coach of the LSU men's basketball team give a speech. One thing stuck out that he said. He said that life revolves around relationships; he went on to add that it is not what you do *to* meet someone but rather, the important part is how you handle your new relationship with someone. What coach Brady meant was meeting new people is great but forging and fostering relationships is how one gets through life. It meant a great deal to me and I am continually forging and fostering relationships with a very diverse population in which I am in contact with.

Another reason I wrote this book is it deserves to be written. What I mean is that I have told this story hundreds of times since it happened some eleven years ago. I can honestly say that I never told it even once when I did not hear at the end of the story that I should write a book or something to make sure others could hear this story. Related to this, I felt remiss to not write the book as a tribute to my new-found friends; the Walden's, the Gilliam's, and the Blount's to name a few. These guys showed me this great time, the least I could do was to put permanently into words, the nice, kind things these folks did for me.

I wrote the book to show the naysayers of the world; we all know the type I am talking about: "you cannot write a book unless you are rich", "you cannot write a book unless you are famous", "you will not find anybody to publish your work", and a myriad of other negative things. Here is proof, you can do what you want if you want, it is that simple.

I have had a lifelong dream of writing something non-fiction just like this book. I am just a regular guy with an extraordinary story to tell. The only regret that I have is that I should have written the book earlier because it has been a true pleasure to do so. It has been a blast! The hard part was just getting started; after that, it went like a breeze. That is my message to all the other regular guys out there who have a story to tell and just dream of telling it and never think that they can tell their story in the form of a book. If I can do it, anyone can do it. One must be hard-headed enough to get started and don't give up until you finish. For me, it was a labor of love and I look very forward to writing many more books in the future.

I would like to thank my dad who got me interested in sports at an early age and more importantly, he liked the Steelers. My two brothers and I were awfully close to our dad and what he liked, we liked. Looking back on growing up, my dad seemed to always show my brothers and I (I am one of identical triplets) how to appreciate the small intricacies of sports. In other words, he taught us that "class" always won. He said that the Steelers would always do at least pretty well because they were a classy team, full of hardworking players and had fine ownership. Other little intricacies he brought to our attention about the Steelers as well as other fine sports teams were to appreciate the field they played on, appreciate the extremely dedicated fans, the storied past of the organization, appreciate the fine coaching jobs done by the head coach and the staff and stuff like that.

I want to thank my wife; Holly has always encouraged me to do my best, to do what I wanted to do. My wife helped me not only to raise a beautiful family but to get through a masters degree and a Ph.D. while taking care of kids, going to work and doing all the other things normal mothers and wives do. As if that is not enough, she has helped me greatly with the writing of this book. I thank you Holly from the bottom of my heart of always being "proud" of me. I, of course, want to thank my three beautiful children for all the support they gave me during this process, showing true patience giving "daddy" time to work. Thanks, Nicolai, Scout, and Cross.

I thank my mother for always being interested. When she saw me writing this book, she would ask questions just to be involved, just to show interest and love to me. She has always been most proud of what I have chosen to do. I thank you mom.

Finally, I cannot thank my two best friends enough; my two brothers. We were raised together, as close as a second skin. Trials and tribulations, ups and downs; through it all we stay close and steadfast to comfort each other and show support for each other. My two brothers, Charles and Sal, have railed on me for the past eleven years to get this book done. Thanks so much, Charles and Sal.

Contents

CHAPTER 1

"Growing Up"

Growing up as one of identical triplets was fun to say the least. We were big on everything that boys are big on; especially sports. Growing up in the 70's was fun for sports fans like us because we loved the Pittsburgh Steelers. Hell, the Steelers were easy to like; in the 70's they beat the hell out of everyone or they came damn close to it, week in and week out! There was also a Louisiana connection because of guys like Terry Bradshaw and Mel Blount. At any rate, if it was pro football we liked it and if it was Steelers football, we loved it. You have to realize how important and impressive the Steelers are if you don't know much about them. They are one of the oldest franchises in the NFL. They were founded in the early 1930's By Mr. Arthur Rooney.

Another thing we liked was horses. We raised, bred, trained, and showed horses as kids and we still do. Our dad, along with us boys befriended a man named Dexter Bates from Bayou Labatrie, Alabama; at least that is where he told us he was from. At the time we knew him, he lived on the outskirts of Slidell, La and was a horse trainer and trader. We bought some saddles and tack from him and saw him at shows and stuff along the way. In the winter of 1976, Dexter called and told us he may have a horse we would be interested in. We got in the truck with our dad and headed to Slidell to see Dexter's horse that was for sale. When we showed up at his place, we saw a big black guy riding a horse around in the arena. We asked our dad who it was and he said: "he looks familiar but I cannot place him" as the man rode the horse closer to where we were parking, dad said: "hey boys, I will be damned, that is Mel Blount of the Pittsburgh Steelers." As you may imagine we were shocked and excited. We were only about 10 or 11 years old but we knew plenty about Mel and the Steelers. As we filed out of the vehicle, it was bitterly cold and windy, we had our jackets on; Steelers Jackets no less. Again, we had no idea that we would run into Mel Blount and still did not know of a connection between Mel and Dexter. When Mel saw us, he got a real kick out of three little guys that looked just alike and he said: "man, ya'll even wore Steelers jackets for me, that's cool." My dad told him that we always wore Steelers jackets and that while we would love to admit wearing them for him, we didn't even know we would see him. It took awhile for him to believe us but we told Mel that we just expected to see Dexter. My dad finally asked Mel why he was there in the first place. He laughed his ass off, got his composure and explained that we were not at "Dexter's Place" but we were at his place. He went on to explain that Dexter worked for him and that Dexter was his trainer. We had no idea!

As I said, it was cold and blustery, Mel said his hands were freezing and my dad piped up and said he had some gloves in the truck that he could use. Dad went and got the gloves which were really nice; leather and rabbit fur insides. Mel attempted to put one on and didn't get them past his knuckles; his hands were as big as a Christmas ham! My dad was a fairly small guy but had pretty big hands and the gloves were really too big for him. I think if they would have fit Mel, I think my dad would have given them to him.

Dexter finally came out of the barn and talked and visited with us; he thought it was funny too that we didn't realize he worked for Mel. It just never came up. Before we got down to the business of horses, Mel mentioned again how proud he was that we had Steelers jackets on and my dad explained to him how all four of us were huge fans of the Steelers. Mel told us that if the Steelers went to the Super bowl the following year, that the four of us would be his guest. He said he would get it done somehow. We were overjoyed to say the least!

We spent the day at Mel's place, riding a few horses, talking, and generally having a good time. We never bought a horse that day either.

I can't remember if it was too expensive, not what we really wanted or what but I know we didn't leave with one. To our sadness, the next season came and went and the Steelers did not play in the big dance so we were not guest of Mel's. As the years past, we often talked about how nice Mel Blount was to us that day and about how much we wished he would have had to make good on that promise.

If you are reading this story you are probably a sports fan of some sort and maybe a Steelers fan. You surely don't have to be either to appreciate the story you are about to read. My point is, is that my incentive for writing the story is simply to show how a normal, everyday person can live a dream with a little luck on your side. Over the years, I have heard several stories that sound amazing or fun and probably like you, I would say to myself: there is no way in hell that I could ever get that lucky! I am living proof that anything can happen to anyone on any day if you are looking at least a little bit. While I am extremely normal in every sense of the word, I will say that I am very talkative, a bit overconfident and extremely polite. Those attributes are just what got me to live the '74 HUSTLE that I lived back in 1999.

CHAPTER 2

"Pittsburgh Week"

To fast forward a couple decades, I was employed by the LSU Agricultural Center as a 4-H youth development agent, working with kids across the state of Louisiana. Each year, a statewide convention of these youth development agents is held and one lucky person is voted upon by his or her peers as the best agent of the year. I was honored and humbled with being voted the best agent in 1999. I was 32 years old, happily married, one beautiful daughter and was on top of my game. Along with this honor, came an all expense paid trip to the national convention for 4-H agents which was held in some major city in the country each year. To my pleasure, the '99 convention was to be held in Pittsburgh.

I had never been to Pittsburgh prior to that time so I was happy to be getting to go, the trip was planned for October which meant it was football season, would the Steelers be playing at home while I was their? I couldn't wait to find out. I did find out and yes, they were playing a Monday night game no less, at home, in Three Rivers Stadium, a storied place to play to say the least, against the Falcons. I felt in my heart that somehow, someway, I would see that game, to live my dream of going to Three Rivers at least once in my life, would it snow during the game too? For a boy from Southeast Louisiana that would be the literal icing on the cake!

The week finally came that I was to go to Pittsburgh with about 20 co-workers and a Supervisor or two. I traveled on a Southwest flight that I swear, laid over in every city up the Eastern seaboard; I finally arrived in downtown Pittsburgh and made my way to my hotel. I had reservations along with my co-workers at the Doubletree downtown, a pretty fancy place for a fellow like me who had not traveled much up until then.

The best thing was that I was a couple days early, affording me the opportunity to look around the city if I wanted. Since I knew there was a Monday night game, I decided to call the ticket office and inquire about a game ticket. When I asked the lady on the phone about purchasing a ticket, she laughed at me! She finally got her composure and told me she was sorry for laughing but that she had worked there many years and had never been asked for a ticket. Puzzled, I asked if I was calling the wrong number or something; she assured me that I was calling the correct place but that tickets were long gone by the time the season rolled around; all of them, every year. She noticed my Southern accent and asked where I was from and I told her New Orleans as I did not think she would know my tiny town, Folsom, a rural town an hour North of New Orleans. She asked me to please not take any offense but that Pittsburgh was different than New Orleans. She went on to explain that I may be able to call the ticket office and get a Saints ticket but that was not going to happen in Pittsburgh. The ticket agent told me that the wait for a single season ticket hovered around 50 years. Finally, she explained that scalping was perfectly legal in Pittsburgh and that I may get a 42 dollar face-value ticket for a couple hundred or so and she wished me good luck. I thanked her for her advice and told her that my plan was to find a ticket around the stadium and pay whatever it took like she told me.

I met with my supervisor to see what our plan was for the week, played around the hotel a while and decided to go down to the street and look around. In the crowded elevator I noticed a distinguished looking man who kind of ran the buttons on the elevator as it was pretty packed and he was the closest guest to the buttons. When he mashed a button for a floor, I noticed he had a ring on his hand that was, without a doubt, a super bowl ring. As people filtered on and off the elevator, we finally got to the ground floor and the two of us ended up alone. I spoke up and told him that I admired his super bowl ring and could I take a closer look at it if he didn't mind. He introduced himself as Mr. Bobby Walden, a Steelers punter from back in the 70's. Actually, the greatest Steelers Punter to ever play. He still owns the record for all time punts at 716. Anyway,he said: "you bet, you can take a closer look and I got another one too" as he held up both fists so I could look at the rings. He said: "you ain't from here, not with that accent" and I said, neither are you, with that southern accent that you have! We both got a chuckle out of that and he told me he lived in Georgia and I told him I was from Southeast Louisiana.

As we wandered out into the lobby from the elevator doors, I jokingly said to him that he had to be one hell of a fan to come out and see his old team play a Monday night game; do you travel up here for all of them I asked? He said "nah, I'm not that big a fan; I am here for a reunion." He went on to tell me that he was there for the 25 year reunion of the 1974 super bowl team of which he was part of. He mentioned that it was ironic because that super bowl was played in New Orleans, where I was from. He said: "you know what I am doing way up here, what are you up here for? I explained to him that I was there for being voted the 4-H agent of the year back in Louisiana and that for that honor, among other things, I got a trip to a national convention of 4-H agents that is in a different city each year, this year, it just happened to be in Pittsburgh. He seemed impressed, he told me that he was quite familiar with the 4-H youth development program as his son had gone through it when he was young.

Bobby asked if I drank beer and I told him that I did; let's get us one in the bar he said and we made our way across the lobby to the bar. You know, I just had a feeling about this guy; he was my kind of guy and I just knew he was going to get something going for me. We found a spot to sit at the bar; a nice place with some atmosphere and a sparse crowd for as big a place as it was. As we drank I told him that I wanted to see the game on Monday night really bad! He understood. I asked Bobby if all the Steelers players from the '74 team were there at the hotel or what the deal with this reunion he spoke of was. He told me that they were, except for a couple. He explained that Terry Bradshaw would not be present because of his T.V. obligations and that Joe Greene would not be present because he was coaching; I think for the Chiefs but not really sure which team he was with at the time and he said everybody else should be there. He told me that Lynn Swan should be there even though he had T.V. obligations because he should be covering the game. I said wait a minute, you mean to tell me that Franco is here, Jack Lambert is here, Rocky is here, coach Noll is here? He said yep and all the others too! I couldn't believe it man, I was in football heaven!

I went on to tell him my Mel Blount story from childhood with the horses and all and I told him how big of a Steelers fan I was. He gave me the rundown on how scarce tickets were and I told him my story of the ticket office. He told me that there was, in fact, a way that I might get to see the game of which I thought his idea would be to scalp a ticket but Bobby had another idea and a damn good one, I would soon find out. He asked me if I remembered Joe Gilliam and I said yes, the backup to Terry (Bradshaw) he said yes. He explained that Joe was kind of the "class clown" back when they played together and that if a deal could be struck in any fashion it would be because of him in most cases. He told me that we had to find Joe to see what he could do, if anything. I then asked Bobby to describe what Joe looked like; explaining to him that I was just a kid when they played and I would never probably recognize him in street clothes 25 years or so after retirement. As Bobby was trying to describe Joe, low and behold, he walks up to the bar across from us and Bobby says: "hell Pete, there's his ass right there"! Bobby summons Joe to come and sit with us and we order another beer and start talking about football, about where we live and stuff like that. I found out that Joe was living in the Nashville area and had been doing some ministerial work with kids and such. Bobby told Joe that I wanted to go to the game and kind of gave him the rundown on how I was a big fan, he explained to him why I was there and all that stuff. Joe told me to give him my room number and give him a couple hours or so to see what he could do. I will never forget that room number; 907, downtown Doubletree hotel in Pittsburgh. He said that he could not promise me anything and that he would see what he could do and call for me later. We sat around a little more as I was mesmerized by the football stories that they caught up on. While we were there, Charles Davis, another Steelers great found us and he entered the conversation. He was living in the Houston, Texas area at the time and was probably one of the nicest guys I have ever met in my life outside of Bobby Walden. He told me with Joe on my side, I was sure to see the game someway; somehow, he said not to worry a bit that I was in good hands. "Mr. Bobby" as I referred to him respectfully, told me "we gonna get you there, don't worry son." I knew he was telling the truth.

When the little party broke up, I hurried to my room to make sure I would catch that phone call, if I was to get one. I called my wife, Holly to tell her the good news. We were only married a few years at the time but she knew well how fond I was of the Steelers and that it was a dream come true just to be in Steel Town, much less actually at a game. I told her about meeting Bobby and Joe and Charles and I also told her that if I never got the first call from Joe and that if I didn't see the game, I felt privileged to have met the Steelers trio and I meant every word of it. I mean really, how many regular walks of life like me get to meet a pro with two rings, look at them up close, have a long conversation with him, meet two more pros of the most fantastic team in the land and drink a beer or two with them? I was privileged, living on borrowed time from that point forward as far as I was concerned.

Well, the phone call finally came, Joe really did call me; I was shocked. I wasn't shocked that I was talking to him but I was shocked that he must have really meant what he said and that he must have found something out, good or bad. In other words, he took the time to think about me, he cared. I would find out how much he cared pretty soon. He talked to me like we were classmates or something. He said, hey Pete, its Joe man, I got some good news and some bad news. He said the '74 team is having a private party tonight here at the Doubletree (It was Saturday before the Monday night game between the Steelers and Falcons) and you cannot come. I laughed and said, why the hell are you telling me that, you teasing me? I said jokingly. He said, no man, just listen a minute, let Jefferson Street Joe tell you the deal. I said ok, go ahead Joe. He said even know you cannot come to the party, I want you there, close by anyway just in case I get something going, in case I can get a deal made for you. He said, I might need you to talk to somebody or something, you never know what may happen. He said are you doing anything tonight? Can you come by the party man? I said hell yes, I will be there. I didn't bother to tell him that I was to be at a mandatory meeting with my coworkers that evening and didn't know how the hell I was going to get out of it but I was, somehow. He said, the deal was that there would be a policeman at the door of the party and that he would be hard to deal with. He said that he would try to arrest me if I was too pushy. He said: these cops up here don't play man, be nice but be firm. He said, tell the cop you are here to see me, tell the cop to come and get me out of the party, tell the cop that you are Mr. Cannizzaro and you are here to see Joe Gilliam for a moment. I had to work fast, the party was approaching fast and I had to get out of an important dinner meeting that I was there for with my coworkers. I didn't know what the hell I was going to do. My supervisor that was at the convention with me was Mr. Terril Faul. Me and Terril were good friends and he was a big sports fan himself, I really hoped he understood. I think I was willing to get fired rather than miss the party. I found Terril in the lobby of the hotel and explained to him what just transpired between me and Joe. He told me that he completely understood my predicament and that if it were him, he would go to the party too. Terril said he would take the heat for me should I get in trouble for not attending the dinner party with him and all my coworkers. Terril is a worrisome guy though; he said if you can't really go to the party why does Joe want you there, what is going on? I told him that I had no idea what was up but come hell or high water, I was going to find out. He laughed and told me to have a good time and good luck with the party that I was not supposed to go to. I knew if I came up dry, with nothing to show from the party that Terril and my other coworkers were going to give me hell about it and I would never live it down.

Well, nighttime finally came and I strolled to the party door and just like Joe said a cop was standing there. When I got in hearing distance, he said in his Pittsburgh accent: "you are in the wrong place big man, this party is private, they ain't signing autographs and you ain't welcome, keep moving." As nice as I could, I said officer, I am a friend of Mr. Joe Gilliam, he asked me to ask you to go and get him for me when I arrived; I am not trying to go in the party, I just want to see Joe like he requested. The policeman said: "yea and I am friends with the fucking president of the United States too; either get out of here or you are going your big ass to jail!" I said I will tell you what; I am not here to make trouble and I cannot make you go and get Joe but with all due respect, the hotel was a public place and I was just going to sit next to the door and wait for Joe. I said you would not throw me out of the hall would you? The cop said: "no, if you want to sit there like a dumbass, be my guest!" So, I slid down the wall, sat on the carpet and let time tick by. After the policeman and I just stared at each other for 30 or 40 minutes or so he finally piped up and said, I will tell you what, I am going in there to find Mr. Gilliam so he can tell me that this is all bullshit and I get to put your ass out of here. I nodded at him as he went through the door to the party praying that he would say my name right, praying that Joe would remember me, praying that Joe gave a damn enough about me out there to say something good. It seemed like forever but the policeman finally came back after being gone for about 10 minutes and he looked at me, stuck out his hand to shake mine and said: "man I owe you an apology, Joe said just hang tight, he will be with you shortly, I am so sorry to have given you shit out here." I said no big deal man, you are just doing your job but thanks for going to see Joe for me. I kind of caught him up on my story to that point, telling him how big of a fan I was, how I was looking for a way into the game and stuff like that. He wished me good luck and agreed that it would be awesome if I got to see a game. He told me that he has seen plenty of them in his day and that no place in the world was like Three Rivers Stadium; I could only hope that I would find out. Believe it or not, me and that policeman sat and talked for three hours or so like old friends. I think we both thought that the party would never end. Just before it ended, the cop said: "hey man, I got something for you" and he handed me a 16" X 20" photograph of the '74 Steelers team. He said: "stick that *don* (local word for down) if your fucking jacket, I was handing these out to the team as they went into the party and there are some extras." He could have handed me a thousand dollars in trade for the photograph and I would not have given it up!

The party finally started to break up, I recognized several players as they came out, a great deal of them with their spouse in tow. To my surprise, I saw my old buddy, Mel Blount come out of the party. I couldn't believe it was really him, after all those years, the memories started to come back about that fateful day in the mid- 70's when me and my family went to his house to see the horse for sale. I had a good feeling he was in the party all the time because there was a coat rack and hat rack out in the hall and on the hat rack was a silver belly hat that just had to be Mel's. I knew he was still an avid horseman and the hat left little to the imagination as to if he was really there. He grabbed his hat and coat and was briskly walking away, he had not aged a bit, could have suited up right then and there for a game, he seemed to be in the epitome of health. As my mind was strolling down memory lane, I quickly jumped to my feet to catch up with him as he strode down a long hall toward the parking lot. I said, hey Mel! and I was at a loss for a moment of what else to say, he looked back at me and never stopped walking and he said, look man, I am not in the mood to sign an autograph, I am tired, I am cold and I am going home. I told him I was not there for an autograph but that I had something to explain to him. He said that I could do all the explaining I wanted as long as I wanted to walk to his car with him. I did not know where to start. I said, Mel, I met you a long time ago at your place in Slidell, LA. He said I am sure you did but I don't remember, that was a long time ago. I said your horse trainer's name was Dexter Bates. He stopped in his tracks and looked at me very quizzically. He said, how do you know that name, do you know where Dexter is? I said that I did not know where he is but that he used to be a friend of mine. He said Dexter was one of my best friends, you sure you don't know where he is? I said that I was sorry but I did not know where Dexter was. I had his attention then. He said I still don't remember meeting you man, sorry. His demeanor was much better now, he knew I was legit, not just wanting an autograph or something like that. I said, Mel, think back, I was one of three triplets who came to your house to look at a horse and we all three had Steelers jackets on, do you recall that? He said: "no way man, is that you? You are one of those little boys? How long ago was that? Your dad tried to lend me some gloves right?" I couldn't believe he would remember such a small detail of our visit way back then. I said, yep, I am one of those little boys and he reached and hugged me. I was in awe. He said: "why didn't you say something man, let's get back inside." I thought to myself that if you would have listened in the first place, we would not have left inside. At any rate, as we strolled back inside the building, I very quickly explained to him what was going on with Joe that he was trying to work something out to get me to the game. He said that, that was great and he would see what he could do as well and he wanted to go back and see Joe for me. I told him that I sure hoped that Joe had not left while we were outside or something like that and he said that

Joe would be the last to leave, don't worry, he will talk to everybody before he leaves. As we got close to the party door, Mel told me to wait a minute, he would be right out. I stood patiently by the door as Mel disappeared. He came out in a few minutes with a man in a three piece suit. The man stuck his hand out and said: "I hear you are a friend of Mr. Blount's is that correct?" I said yes, proud that Mel must have told him we were friends. He said that any friend of Mel's was a friend of his. He said: "Hello Mr. Cannizzaro, I am Dan Rooney, I own this team." You could have knocked me over with a feather; here I was talking to Mr. Rooney, the owner of the Pittsburgh Steelers, man alive! With Mel standing by, I gave Mr. Rooney a quick synopsis as to why I was in Pittsburgh, about me and Joe, me and Mel, that I met Mel as a child and that I visited earlier in the day with Bobby Walden, Joe Gilliam, and Charles Davis. He then said: you know what the shame is, is that if this were a Sunday game instead of a Monday game that I would be in his suite sitting in a recliner watching the game with him but that since it was a Monday game, only immediate family could be there. He explained that it was not his rule but the rule of the league and he had to abide by it. He wished me good luck and said, just like everybody else so far, as long as you have Joe working for you, I really think you will get into the game.

Well, Mel was just right, Joe would be very last to leave the party. He finally came out and pulled me to the side. He told me he had a deal. I quickly said that any ticket would be fine, even in the nosebleed section. He told me to stop talking about tickets, that everybody already explained to me that there are no tickets available to a Steelers game. I settled down to listen to his deal. He said: look, I talked to our old public relations guy about you and told him that I needed to help you out. Yes, he said he *needed* to help me; I would find out what he truly meant later on. He said that he needed me in the Doubletree lobby at 3:00p.m. on Monday afternoon as I was going to be the personal guest of the '74 super bowl Steelers team and that I was to board a bus with the team and go to the game with them and that other details would be worked out later. I actually asked Joe if he was joking with me; he assured me that it was not a joke and that I was his guest and the guest of the other players too. I couldn't believe my ears!

The good news was that I was going to the game with the '74 team, the bad news was that I was going to miss yet another important meeting that I was supposed to attend with my LSU Ag Center coworkers. I knew I would work it out, somehow, I would get by this or I would surely let them fire me in trade of going to the game with the '74 team. I say that with tongue firmly planted in cheek as I knew I wouldn't be fired but I knew I was going have to sweet talk my way out of a second meeting that I was supposed to attend. I worked for a great place though; I knew all would be well.

I found the nearest pay phone and called home to tell my wife, Holly and called my brothers as well to let them in on what was going on. Keep in mind, it was the middle of the night and I was going to wake up everyone that I was calling but I did not care a bit and knew they would not care either. My wife was like most wives; worried something had happened since I was calling so late and when she found out that I was alright, wanted to know what I was calling in the middle of the night for. I explained to her what the deal was; what Joe had told me. She could not believe it; not appreciating football or the Steelers as much as I did but she knew it was a dream come true for me. When I got in touch with my brothers, they were ecstatic! They couldn't believe the I was actually going to Three Rivers Stadium and was going to see the Steelers play ball and better than that, was the guest of the '74 team. Keep in mind, they knew as much about football and those famous players as I did and they sure seemed excited for me and were going to try to see me on T.V. when the game was telecast on Monday night.

I was just kind of in a cloud until Monday afternoon rolled around, visited with some coworkers, found some good food in the city and stuff like that. It was also cold and lightly snowing on and off during those couple days and that was right up my alley; at that time, you could have counted on one hand how much snow I had seen. All the locals were kind of complaining about it as I would have been too I guess if I were raised in a climate like that.

Chapter 3

"Game Day"

Monday finally rolled around and it was a dreary, snowy and gray day out; just what I had hoped for! I got dressed for the game at about noon not wanting to be anywhere near late to the lobby. I wore a ball cap, sweatshirt, some jeans and my boots, I was ready to roll. I thought I would just tough out the weather because I didn't bring a heavy jacket, just a couple blazers as most of my trip was to be spent indoors. As I was leaving the room I noticed something in my hanging bag that looked odd; it was a goose down jacket that belonged to my brother, Charles. He had asked if I wanted to bring it along but I told him no in fear of something happening to it; it was his favorite and it was expensive. I smiled to myself knowing that he put the damn thing in my bag at the last second so I would be prepared. I slipped it on, damn happy that he put it in my bag because I would most assuredly need it. I made my way down to the lobby about an hour and a half early and I am glad I did as several of the current players (current in 1999) were milling around and talking to fans. I learned that the current team used the hotel for pre-game meetings and it was coincidental that the '74 team was there too. I thought: "sweet for me!" I found a large dish on the counter of the check-in desk with just a few home-made cookies in it. I could tell that there were plenty of cookies a few minutes before my arrival. I was glad to get a couple because I was hungry and sure as hell was not

15

leaving to eat and miss anything. Over my shoulder I noticed the great Jerome Bettis; the Bus. I quickly walked over and said hello to him and he gladly shook my hand. He told me they always came to the hotel before home games and I could tell he was looking at the cookies in my hand. He smiled and mentioned that he came almost daily when he could because of the good cookies the hotel provided; I thought that was as funny as hell. He said that he was signing autographs and such and didn't get any cookies that day. I offered one of mine to him and he smiled really big and said thanks and he gobbled it up! I told him how big a fan I was and that I was honored to share a cookie with him and he told me that he was glad that I was attending the game and wished me luck. Coming off the elevator was the Slash or current Quarterback, Cordell Stewart. He had little boys covering him, wanting autographs, pictures and anything they could get in the way of attention. I managed to squeeze in and get a hello in and he quickly signed an autograph on a hotel napkin for me. Pretty shortly, the players left for the stadium and some charter buses pulled right up to the door outside for the '74 team. It was snowing hard outside, I was in awe of my surroundings and what was going on with me. Life for me at that moment couldn't have been better. The '74 players started to slowly trickle out of the elevator and into a bus. A substantial amount of them had their wife with them so it didn't take long for a bus or two to fill up and leave for Three Rivers which was an eleven block run as I was told. I was getting apprehensive waiting on Joe and Mel. Joe told me to wait on him and Mel and we would board the bus together. The minutes passed and more and more people boarded the remaining buses and they were filling up but I didn't see Mel or Joe. I began to think that maybe I missed them somehow. Maybe they thought I decided to not come or maybe something happened to me and I couldn't make it and they left me. Hell, I was in a pinch and didn't know what the hell to do. When the last bus seemed to be close to full and I had not seen my two buddies, I decided to board the bus and see what would happen.

Mel Blount, myself, and Joe Gilliam at the Doubletree Hotel

As I approached the first step, a man in a suit and mirror sunglasses put his hands on my chest (he was a step above me already on the bus) and told me that the bus was for '74 players and their families and that if I didn't want trouble to back off. I looked at him and told him I was the personal guest of the team and was attending the game with them. He chuckled and said: "yeah, bull fucking shit big man" and he said it kind of loud. At that moment, to my surprise and relief, Joe and Mel were making their way out of the lobby and onto the bus too, right behind me. Joe spoke up: "hey man, that is Mr. Cannizzaro and he is with us, let him on…now!" the man apologized profusely to me as I boarded and I told him not to worry about it and that if the tables were turned, I would not have believed him either. He said, well I am going to make it up to you sir, follow me to your seat. He led me three quarters of the way down the aisle and said: "sit here between two NFL Hall of Famers, meet Mr. Dwight White and Jack Lambert" I could not believe my ears! I was shaking hands and sitting next to one of the greatest middle linebackers ever, Jack Lambert. They welcomed me and said that they heard about me and were glad to see me there. I felt like a king right then. Mel and his wife sat a few rows away from me and Joe's wife did as well. The bus seemed to be all filled up so Joe said he would stand and that it was all good because he wanted to walk and talk to people anyway. When Joe came close to where I was sitting, I thanked him for all he had done and asked what I owed him. He told me that I had to have a good time and that would be payment enough and he explained that he didn't know what was going to transpire when we got to the stadium. He explained that, at worst, he would get me into Three Rivers and that at that point, I would be kind of on my own and probably would be able to find a seat in the high section or somewhere where there was a no-show. I told him that, that sounded great and that I couldn't wait. Mel Blount, being playful and serious at the same time, loudly interjected: "You are not about to leave this man out in the cold! He is not going to find a no-show seat; he is with us man!" Joe explained that he had done all he could to this point and I argued with him saying that what they all had done to this point was more than enough; more than I ever dreamed of. Mel would hear none of it and Joe started to get fired up, saying o.k. what do we do when we get there Mel? Mel said he would handle that and that he (Joe) needed to keep his reputation as a deal maker on the positive side by making sure I got to see a great time-with them.

As we pulled into the stadium and up to a gate, a suited gentleman boarded the bus and kind of de-briefed all the team members and wives; explaining to them that the fans knew exactly what was going on; they knew that the '74 team was coming for a special 25 year anniversary event at halftime. He further explained that if they could run, to run into the stadium because the fans were going to be raucous, pulling on their clothes, asking for autographs and the like. Once the man got all the preliminaries out of the way he explained the good stuff. He said that the Steelers organization spent $125,000 on a pre-game party with all the trimmings. He said that the party included prime steaks, huge shrimp, all sorts of other foods and plenty to drink. He explained that we had about 4 hours until game time and before the party we would tour the locker room and other facilities inside the stadium. Finally, he said all players and family members needed a press pass to be able to come inside and to be able to amble about freely during the game. The players and family members also learned that there was a special, small set of portable bleachers at the corner of the end zone closest to the stadium meant for them. As the players and spouses filed off the bus, they were presented with a red, diamond shaped pass around their necks; the all famous press pass; a pass that lets you go anywhere you want on the field or stadium. When I got up I followed Mel, behind me in the aisle was Joe. When Mel reached the front of the bus, he bent down, got his pass put on his neck and he moved aside to let me get one. The man looked at me, looked at Mel kind of puzzled and in unison, Mel and Joe said: "he is with us!" the man just nodded yes and slipped a pass on my neck! I was in heaven.

I really got an appreciation for how famous and well-liked these guys are when we waded through the crowd for the short distance from the bus to the facility. As the man told us, the fans cheered, yelled, asked for autographs and were just euphoric about the '74 champs being there. Hell, I turned down giving an autograph six times on the way in; they thought I was a former player too! Talk about making a man feel good. We moved inside and took the promised tour of the locker rooms, other behind-the-scene areas of the famed Three Rivers Stadium. Of course, the former players liked seeing the "digs" but were not nearly as impressed as I was. They had spent time in locker rooms most of their lives, I, on the other hand, had not ever seen anything like it. I was in awe.

We finally moved into the party. It was a big room with a bar, tables, food everywhere, a couch or two; set up like a normal looking barroom except that out of a set of glass back doors we the field! The room opened up just beyond an end zone of the field. I grabbed up pieces of paper, napkins, anything I could find to start gathering autographs from all the players.

Head Coach Chuck Noll.

Roy Gerela, placekicker.

John"Frenchy" Fuqua, running back. The intended target for
Terry Bradshaw's pass that resulted in the Immaculate Reception
(top) (bottom) Lionel Taylor, wide receiver coach.

DoubleTree
Hotel
PITTSBURGH

1000 PENN AVENUE
PITTSBURGH, PENNSYLVANIA 15222-3873
412/281-3700

Dwight White, defensive end and member of the famed "Steel Curtain",(top) (bottom)
is Ernie Holmes, defensive lineman, another member of the famed "Steel Curtain".

Bobby Walden, punter and the man who started my whole experience with the team (top) (bottom) another autograph of the great Dwight White.

Mel Blount, the great cornerback with his NFL Hall of Fame induction year.

Jack Lambert, middle linebacker, maybe the best to ever play the position.

My press pass to get into the game; front side middle top: John McMakin, #89, tight end. top right corner, Ed Bradley, linebacker. Bottom left, the great receiver, John Stallworth. Bottom right, unknown player.

23

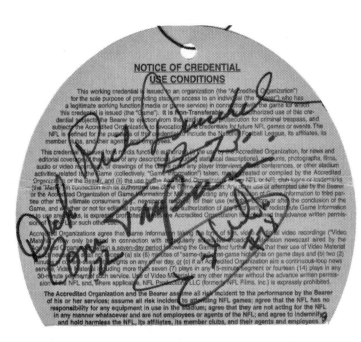

Back of pass-top center, Rick Druschel, guard # 73. bottom
left- Dick Conn, #22, defensive back. Center middle- Tony
Parisi, field manager. Bottom center, Dwight White.

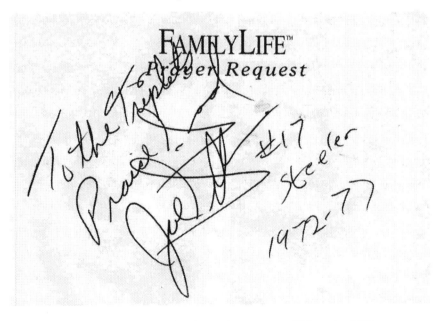

FAMILYLIFE™
Prayer Request

M favorite of all, signed: "to the triplets praise god" from Joe Gilliam,
#17, quarterback with his years as a Steelers member also listed).

I was reacquainted with the man who started it all for me; Bobby Walden as well. He gave me a warm handshake and a pat on the back and said he was glad I worked it out.

During the party, I listened and sidled up to as many conversations as I could as I filled up on giant shrimp and crown and seven with a twist of lime; the finest party I had ever seen with a guest list second to none. I talked to Mel about the horse business of which he is still active in today. We also talked about his two homes for wayward boys in Georgia and in Pennsylvania and just kind of caught up on quarter horse news and football news. Joe was a stellar host, he guided me around, helping me get my autographs, making jokes with his old buddies, and being happy to be alive. He nodded me over to talk to the great Jack Lambert. It seemed that Mr. Lambert wanted to talk a little and I did too.

Me and Bobby Walden, the very first Steelers player I met and the one who made my fantastic event even possible.

Peter Cannizzaro

From left to right: Mel Blount (cowboy hat) John Stallworth (bald, drink in hand) Jack Lambert with coat and tie and Jack Ham on the far right with the cap on

I asked Jack how it was that he always seemed to have his front teeth knocked out after a game. He laughed modestly and told me that, it was just the way he played. I told him that, I had no problem understanding that from watching him play but I explained that I didn't understand how it happened with the face mask on the helmet, no matter how hard you played. He told me in a matter-of-fact manner that if you hit someone hard enough, the mask was meant to be bent in toward the face and not break. I told him that I thought that was amazing; amazing that he would try to hit that hard every play. He told me that if he didn't knock a tooth or two out that he didn't feel as successful after a game. Jack Lambert went on to explain that his state of mind just changed when he crossed into the chalk lines of a football field. He told me that he knows some people think he may have been the best middle linebacker to play or at least one of the top few of which I totally agreed with but he said he didn't know much about all of that but that he thought he was that good when the starting whistle blew and that is what counted. I asked him about his retirement days and asked what he had been up to and he told me that he was a game warden in the Lancaster, PA area. I thought to myself that I would hate to meet up with a Jack Lambert type of guy in the woods; with a gun! I moved around the party some and noticed a nice looking gent with a mustache of which I did not recognize. I knew

26

he was a former player but I did not know which one. I introduced myself to him and he did the same; he was Rick Druschel, a former guard that only played pro ball for the 1974 season. He and his wife were both really nice and invited me to sit with them. I kind of gave Rick the rundown as to how I made it to the game that day. He was glad I was there; he told me that he coached high school ball at a Pittsburgh high school and that he was good friends with Coach Cowher. I was impressed to say the least. We ate and drank a little and Rick had a suggestion. He told me that I would probably never get a chance to see Three Rivers Stadium again of which I readily agreed. He then asked me if I wanted to "sneak" outside for a few minutes and go to the middle of the field to see if we could chat with Bill Cowher. I asked him if we would be alright doing this; he playfully flicked my press pass with his thick middle finger and said: "we own the place right now buddy." How could I argue with that? We hit the double glass doors to find a screaming stadium full of fans, a light snow falling and cold as all hell. He looked at me and said: "let's run out to the fifty like we own the place and see if we see Bill ok?" I followed him on the best jog I ever had in my life. I got to jog out on the field hearing thousands of fans cheering and making all sorts of noise. I smiled as I got the feeling that NFL players were sure lucky to feel what they feel sometimes. Rick hugged coach Cowher and introduced me; Coach seemed glad to see me and said that he hoped I had a helluva good time while at the stadium. Coach Cowher introduced me to one of his assistant coaches named Mike Archer. Coach Cowher, knowing that I was from Louisiana, said that I should enjoy meeting Mr. Archer since he used to be the head coach at LSU. I was also freezing my ass off because I forgot my jacket inside the party. After Coach Archer went back to work, Coach Cowher told me that my press pass would allow me on the sidelines if I wanted to be there and that I should stay out of the way of him and the team. He playfully quipped that if I wanted to get in the way, get in the way of Coach Glanville on the other side. Coach bid me a goodbye and we ran back into the party.

When we got back to the party, it was kind of winding down and folks started making their way to the special bleachers for the '74 team and families. I got another crown and seven with a twist of lime and headed out the door too. The game was still a good ways from starting and I was gawking at everything I could. What was neat about going outside was that I really got a chance to meet more players as they mingled and relaxed. Something funny happened; Blount went to sit down in the special bleacher/sitting section for players and families and he kind of slipped and fell. He was laughing hard when it happened and he just about fell in John Stallworths' lap!

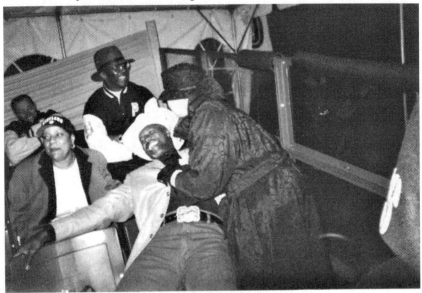

Mel Blount with a little "mishap" slipping in bleachers with his wife helping and laughing along with him

I met the defensive greats; Charles Davis, Ernie Holmes and Dwight White. These guys were a big part of that great defense that Pittsburgh put on the field. Charles and the others but especially Charles treated my like family.

Charles told me not to go sit down yet, he told me to walk around and soak it all up and soak it up I did! I also got a chance to see the "Bus" Jerome Bettis again as he strode around the field in his warm ups. I was so proud to see him again and he seemed happy to take a moment or two to talk to me. The neatest thing was that he was surprisingly short; under six feet but that the top if his legs looked like he was standing in two city garbage cans! His legs were freakishly big! I walked around and looked and listened and enjoyed as much as I could.

Me and the "big man" Charles Davis

The great Jerome Bettis better known as the "The Bus"warming up before the game

As the game started to get underway, I started getting cold and I finally realized it was snowing lightly. At that time, that was a big deal because you could only count on one hand how many times I had seen snow in my life. I was amazed that it took me so long to appreciate the snow; I was so enamored with the pre-game and all the other stuff going on, I could not believe it took me so long to appreciate the snow. Since I was getting cold and started actually thinking realistically, I went to hunting my jacket. I found it over close to the door where the party had been going on and I hurried to put it on. I smiled inside that I had the nice goose down jacket to wear. My brother Charles insisted that I put it into my luggage just prior to leaving on the trip. I didn't have a nice looking heavy jacket, only seldom needing one in Southeast Louisiana. I was damn glad my brother had a good one that I actually argued with him about taking along. I slipped in on and quickly zipped it up. At that moment I told myself: "you dumb ass, you don't have any gloves, your hands going to fall off!" I jammed my hands into the jacket pockets and low and behold, Charles left a glove in each pocket by mistake and I was the lucky finder of a much-needed gift. I thought that that was kind of fateful that the gloves were accidentally left in the jacket pockets. I happily slipped them on. At that moment, another very important fact came to mind; I say to myself: "hey dumb ass, no camera!" How the hell can you come to a Steelers game with no camera?" I literally almost cried; I even remembered that I saw some throw-a-way cameras for sale at the hotel store and it never crossed my mind to buy one. How the hell stupid can a fellow be I thought. I swear on my dads grave, I bent down to pick up a pen that fell off my ear, causing my jacket to tighten up some as I bent over and I felt something in the inside vest pocket of the jacket and it even kind of hurt my chest. I stood up straight and reached in; you guessed it, my boy Charles left (by accident no doubt) a throw-a-way camera in the top inside pocket of the jacket he lent me. I can't make this shit up. I jumped up and down like I scored a touchdown I was so happy about the camera. I looked at the top of the camera and it only had one picture taken on it which left me 23 chances to get some pictures of my memorable experience. If that is not fate than nothing is. I realized right then and there that I was meant to be in Three Rivers Stadium at that moment and watching that game and hanging out with my newfound friends. An older gentleman started making his way down the sideline toward the special seats, I could not believe my eyes; Head Coach Chuck Noll was just steps away from where I stood. I couldn't believe it man, the coach of all coaches. He walked up stuck his hand out and said: "Hello sir, who are you?" I told him my name and a 30 second version of why I was there and then asked him if he minded us taking a picture together.

Maybe the best NFL coach ever; the great Chuck Noll and myself

He said that he would not only take one with me but that he would be honored; yes, honored. That is the treatment I got from all these great, great players and people within the past and present Steelers organization. I got somebody to hold and shoot my cardboard camera at me and coach and the picture came out great; one of my favorite pictures from the event for sure. I was feeling high on life; walked up and down each sideline, ending up on the 30 or so yard line of the home team. I watched several plays as the game went kind of back and forth for a while. Just then, a middle aged lady in a stadium type uniform came walking out of the double doors where I had partied with the team. She had her eye on me, a scowled look on her face and I began to panic. I wondered what the hell I did wrong; did I step on the field? Did I get in coach Cowher's way? Did I say something wrong to someone? I was scared to death and just knew she was coming to kick my ass right off the field and out of the stadium. It seemed like hours before she reached me, when she did, she said in her gruff northeastern way: "Were you the

31

one drinking crown and seven in the party?" I stammered out a "yes mam" , showing as much southern charm as I could and she said: "I ain't that goddamn old, don't call me mam! I just want to know if you want another drink because you seem to be having so much fun. I could not believe my ears, she wasn't kicking my ass out, she was comforting me for Christ sake! She showed back up shortly with not one but two crown and seven drinks, twist of lime included in big Styrofoam cups and she bid me a goodbye. I was in hog heaven, nothing could have topped the time I was having. Just as I started to think that things were somewhat normal and I was growing used to my euphoric trip I felt a tap on my shoulder. That tap came from none other than Mr. Franco Harris.

He stuck his hand out and as we shook hands he told me that some of the other guys told him my story and he wanted to meet me. You heard it right, he wanted to meet me! We stood shoulder to shoulder for a little while and the Steelers were on a drive, getting close to scoring, me and Franco headed down toward the end zone as to not miss the action. Shortly after, Richard Huntley caught a touchdown pass from Kordell Stewart to score the only touchdown of the game. What made it a touchdown of a lifetime for me was that I turned to Franco, he turned to me and we high fived each other as if we had it planned for years. I literally got a tear in my eye; how many people can say that they have got a high five from one of the best mail carriers in the history of the game. It goes without saying that it was pretty damn hard to pay attention to the game because I was so enamored by all the other stuff going on at the time.

As half time approached a man walked around with souvenir programs and was handing them out to all the '74 players and their family members; that included me too. I quickly thumbed through it and found a centerfold layout of the '74 team and started asking for autographs.

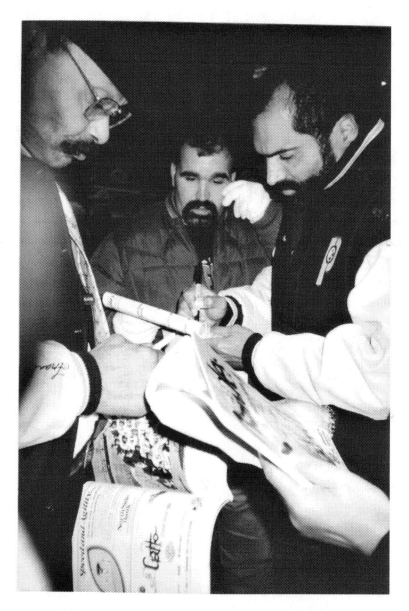

Two greats, Joe Gilliam and Franco Harris signing my program, me
in the middle and wiping a tear of disbelief from my eye.

**My centerfold program picture of the '74 team with
many, many autographs of the team and staff.**

The players were doing the same thing as I was, milling around getting their teammates to sign their books. I took an opportunity to get several photos with my camera of some of the greats from the team. The folks were so nice to take pictures for me; I was amazed. I got a lady (a players wife I am sure) to get a picture of me and the great Ernie Holmes, Charles Davis and L.C. Greenwood and I was lucky enough to get a shot of Roy Gerela walking around and I caught John Stallworth signing a banner.

Me and the great Ernie Holmes.

A great candid shot of the great Roy Gerela.

A great candid shot of the great John Stallworth signing his
autograph to a banner with Joe Gilliam looking on.

Charles Davis on my right and L.C. Greenwood on
my left. Two "big units" from the team.

A few minutes into the signing session, the same man showed up with jackets and caps for all the former players. The jackets were the letterman style jackets with leather sleeves with a wool body. The players immediately started getting each other to sign the sleeves of the jackets. I quickly realized that the leather sleeves were on purpose-made for signing. Each jacket and hat came with a nice brand new sharpie pen as well. Well, I am sad to say that I was not on the jacket list but I went ahead and asked for one anyway; what the hell, everything else was falling into place so I thought I should ask. The gentleman told me that while he did not feel he had an extra one he would surely look for either a jacket and/or a cap. True to his word, he showed up several minutes later empty handed. He told me he was sorry but just could not come up with anything. I told him not to worry and that I appreciated his efforts. He went on to tell me that it was a shame that I could not get a jacket because just having the jacket without the autographs but with the big super bowl patch would make the limited edition jacket worth thousands (not that I would have ever parted with one should I have gotten one) he finally added that with the autographs the jacket could be sold for no telling how much or basically priceless. The jacket with autographs would probably fetch piles of money from a fanatic collector. Again, mine would never have been for sale. I was glad that the man thought about me and at least tried to fine me one. I did have my program all filled with autographs.

Halftime finally rolled around and that is when the big party started; the time when each and every player off the '74 roster got to go out on the field and have the fans yell and scream for them. You could only imagine how it sounded when Jack Lambert walked out; the sounds of the thousands of people, the light snow falling; a true Steelers night to remember. It came to be Mel Blounts' turn to go on the field. As cold as it was, wind blowing, snow falling, he removed his jacket to reveal a snug black short sleeved shirt along with his silver belly Stetson cowboy hat. He looked like he could have played that night he was in such good shape. He asked me to hold his jacket while he ran on the field; I was only happy to do so. I asked him if he was sure he wanted to go in short sleeves as it was quite cold. He said: "man, these fans remember the young and tough Blount I can't go out there with a jacket like I can't take the cold!" with that he made his memorable jog on out and the crowd busted in half for him. On his return he told me to give him that damn jacket; he was freezing his butt off! But as promised, the crowd saw the stealth, tough, badass cornerback that they came to love in the 70's. As you might imagine, all the players got really big applause, some of the more known or famous players received more; like Lambert and Blount as I mentioned but they also went berserk for Franco, Stallworth, Swann and many more. Even head coach Chuck Knoll made his mid field stroll and the fans appreciated him to say the least. I felt almost guilty as I got to shake hands with the players as they came off the field and the folks in the stands were held at bay, not nearly as lucky as I was. A touching moment for me was when it was Bobby Waldens' turn to go out he not only asked his son to hold his jacket but he *gave* the jacket to his boy. I watched that young man who was around my age slide on that Steelers jacket with the pride of a true man; a man admiring his fathers past works. It really touched my heart. I lost my dad several years prior to that night and I was proud for the young Walden to experience this with his dad.

After halftime, I stowed my program safely inside my jacket and strolled the field feeling 10 feet tall and bullet proof, mingling idly with the former players, some of their family members and whoever would give me the time of day. Hell, everybody wanted to talk to me; here I was standing, sitting, talking to and visiting with perhaps the greatest football team to ever take the field and it all happened because of a few players who still knew how to be unselfish and help an average guy like me on any given day. During the third and fourth quarters, players started to leave slowly as a bus would leave every twenty or thirty minutes or so for those who were tired, cold or both. Of course, several players stayed till the end of the game as did I. I would never have even thought of leaving early; they were going to have to kick my big ass out of the stadium for me to leave.

The game finally ended and the Steelers were going to win the game. The score ended at 13 to 9. Somebody yelled that the last bus was not far from leaving and you could count the players on one hand that needed to take that bus. I knew I needed to catch the bus but wanted to talk to Joe Gilliam before anything else. I saw Dick Conn and Ed Bradley as they made their way to the bus. I told them to tell the driver that I would be there as soon as I could; telling them I needed to thank Joe in case he didn't get back on the bus. They said not to worry because the traffic would be tied up for a long time and the bus would be there for some time to come. Relieved, I found Joe on the sidelines talking to someone and when he saw me he eased over my way and said: "I hope you had a good time big man, if you are ever In the Nashville area, you have a place to stay." I told him that, that was most appreciated but that I wanted to thank him from the bottom of my heart for doing what ever he did to get me to the game that night. I added that outside of the birth of my only daughter at the time, that the night of October 25, 1999 was the best night of my life. He then thanked me. I was confused, I said: "no Joe, I am thanking you for making my dream come true" and he said: "and I am thanking you for making mine come true too". Totally confused I told him I didn't know what he was talking about but that if I owed him anything at all to just say the word. He pulled me over to a bench and he sat, his wife a few yards away and he motioned for me to sit as well. He looked me in the eyes and said exactly this: "Pete my man, I have been up and I have been down, I have eaten in the white house and I have eaten from the garbage cans of this very city. My ups and downs taught me several things but the biggest thing it taught me was that when someone asks for help and it is within your limits, not only do you help them, you are obliged to help them, you asked me to get you to the game, you were not pushy, you were able to show me just how important it was that you make the game and I quickly realized that getting you here was within my limits and not only did I want to do it, I had to do it. The good lord puts us here to help not only ourselves but to help others too. So, Pete that is why I said thanks to you." I just sat and looked at him as his eyes filled with tears and mine had already spilled over. I reached out to shake his hand and he ignored my outstretched hand and hugged me. After that hug we shared I shook his hand and started to walk away, his wife, tears streaming down her face hugged me as well and reiterated that I had a place to stay in Nashville and told me to have a safe trip home and that she loved me. I decided right then and there that I just talked to one of the best men that the good lord ever made. I just talked to a man among men. As if all this was not enough, he asked if he could give me another autograph but wanted to add my brothers to it since I had told him all about being an identical triplet. I was truly honored for him to give me an autograph "to the triplets" of which me and my brothers treasure to this day.

Chapter 4

"The Ring"

On a lighter note, I made my way to the bus to find a driver, Ed Bradley, Dick Conn and myself and nobody else on the bus. I took a seat across the isle from the guys as they welcomed me aboard. The driver told us to sit tight, get comfortable, and we would still be on the bus an hour or more to go our eleven blocks back to the double tree hotel. He even said that he wouldn't be offended if we decided to take a cab as it may be slightly quicker. We all decided that sitting on the bus and just relaxing would be better than hailing a cab and that the bus was comfortable and warm. I saw that Ed Bradley was wearing his super bowl ring and I asked him if he could lean my way so I could take a better look. He told me he would do me one better and took it off and handed it to me. I turned on my reading light to look at all the words on the ring, all the detail of it; I wanted to learn exactly what it looked like before I handed it back. Several minutes later I went to hand it back to him and he held his hand up as if to stop me. He quipped "I see that college ring on your hand, take that off and wear mine a while, you are used to big rings, when else would you have the chance to wear a super bowl ring?" I could only agree, quickly taking my college ring off and pushing it in my pocket and putting his on. It fit perfect! As we eased down the road in the bus through the traffic, me marveling at the door knob on my hand with my trusty overhead reading lamp, Ed said he wanted to tell me and Dick a story about his ring since we would be there a while. He told us that he damn near lost his ring forever several years back. He and his wife were going out one night and when he looked for his ring it was nowhere to be found. After much hollering and cussing and turning the house over to no avail, his little boy finally figured out what all the fuss was over and explained to his dad that he traded the ring to a boy at school for a marble! Of course, the boy had no idea of the rings importance or value. If memory serves me, he was just like maybe 5 years old or so. At any rate, the little fellow could not remember the other child's name in which he made the trade with. With that news, Ed insisted that his wife call the boys teacher right then and there, wake her up if need be and figure out what the deal was. The little boy was able to describe the other boy and the teacher said she thought she knew who it may be. The teacher, knowing full well the gravity of the situation quickly drove over to the Bradley's and they all went to the home of the other little boy. When they arrived, they had to explain what they were all doing at the peoples house in the middle of the night and the parents at least appreciated fully what was at stake. They asked their own son if he made such a trade and he assured him that he had. The big question was where is the ring? The poor boy forgot where he put it and did not even remember if he still had it! The four parents along with the teacher turned this house upside down too and to no avail, no ring. After a couple hours of looking, the Bradley family was headed home, heads held low in defeat. Almost to the car the man of the house says: "wait, the sandbox has not been checked!" He ran for a flashlight and headed to the corner of the yard and with a quick shine saw nothing. Ed asked him to maybe check the box in the morning when it was light; saying that to find it in a sandbox was highly unlikely anyway. The little boy finally remembered something, he ran to his dump truck in the sandbox and on the driver seat of the toy truck sat the ring of all rings. It was found; Ed has his ring in his hand. Ed finished up the story by saying that the next day he took the ring straight to the bank and got a safety deposit box and that the deposit box would be the new home for the ring from then on.

By the end of the story, we were just getting back to the hotel. We shook hands, thanked the driver and unloaded. I wearily made my way into to doubletree looking forward to a bed. It was like 1 o'clock in the morning and I had a big day to say the least. Ed and Dick went their way and I went mine. The lobby was quite large, we were some fifty feet apart and Ed stopped, turned and hollered in a playful but anxious way: "Hey man, give me my damn ring back, I can't stand to lose it again!" It seemed that since I was used to wearing rings, I forgot to give his back. The three of us got a big laugh and I handed Ed his ring and told him how much of a thrill it was to wear it. As we parted ways, the twenty or so people from Louisiana that I came on the trip with were waiting for me near the bar area and clapped for me as I headed toward them. They were so proud for me and I was so proud that they stayed up for me and to welcome me "home" after my big day. I realized that I had just got to experience one of the finest fan experiences that a man could have experienced.

After I got to my room, I thought I was ready to go to bed but I was still stoked about what had happened. I decided to call my two brothers and relive the experience with the two other biggest Steelers fans in the world. I had no cell phone in those days so I could not call from the game or anything. All they knew for sure was that I was at the game because they actually saw me on television a couple times. I think I finally lay down at around 3 o'clock in the morning.

Make no mistake, several Steelers made this night possible for me as you can see from this story but without my chance meeting with Bobby Walden on the elevator in the Doubletree where we all stayed and without his good nature and giving me much more than the time of day, not if this would be possible. Bobby Walden like Joe Gilliam, a true man among men.

The next day and the next several to follow, I tried to come back down to earth and get focused on why I was really in Pittsburgh which was for a really educational and enjoyable conference with several thousand people who did 4-H youth development work like I did. News travels fast though, it seemed that everywhere I went, every person I talked to knew who I was. They would say, hey, you are the lucky guy who made it to the Steelers game back on Monday right? Then they would say how the hell did you manage such a thing? As you might imagine, I re-told my story to whoever would listen for as long as they would listen.

CHAPTER 5

"Steelers History"

The teams' original name was the Pittsburgh Pirates, they were a member of the Eastern Division of the NFL which consisted of 10 teams back then. Mr. Rooney is considered one of the pioneers of the sporting world, Art Rooney passed away in the summer of 1988 after having a stroke at the age of 87. "The Chief" as he was affectionately known, is enshrined in the Pro Football Hall of Fame and is remembered as one of Pittsburgh's greatest people. Mr. Rooney lived his life on the North side of the city not far from Three Rivers Stadium.

Rooney was an exceptional athlete himself, he held middleweight and welterweight titles from the AAU Boxing Championships and was named to the U.S. Olympic Boxing Team in 1920. Although he did not follow up on the boxing opportunity but did play minor league baseball from 1920 to 1925 before his career fell short due to an arm injury. Before marrying in 1931 and having five fine sons, he played semi-pro football for several teams in the Pittsburgh area. Art Rooney was inducted into the NFL Hall of Fame in 1964 for his contributions to the Steelers and to the league.

By the middle 1960's much of the operation of the Steelers were being handed over to Mr. Rooney's eldest son, Dan. Dan was named President of the Team in 1975 and was inducted himself into the NFL Hall of Fame in 2000. Father like son, Dan Rooney was extremely active with not only his team but with the NFL until 2002 when he stepped down and handed the head job to his son, Art Rooney II.

Make no mistake, the Steelers has had some hard times, not always being as successful as they have been in the last 35 or 40 years. In the 1930's Rooney founded the team and watched them struggle in its first seven years of existence as it won only 22 games in that time span with a whopping five head coaches. Rooney often took his team to cities around the country to play in towns that did not have pro football teams and to try to stay away from competition including baseball and college football.

In 1938 Mr. Rooney signed the first "big money" player; Byron White signed a contract for $15,800. White led the league in rushing in his first year and became the NFL's most illustrious alumni. White followed his football career with a 31 year career as a Justice of the United States Supreme Court before retiring in 1993.

In 1940 Rooney changed the name of the team to the Steelers which represents the heritage of the city. In 1942 the team got its first winning record under the tutelage of head coach Walt Kiesling. In 1946 Rooney hired the legendary coach from the University of Pittsburgh, Jock Sutherland. In Southerland's second year at the helm, the Steelers reached a record of 8-4. Also in 1947, the Steelers lost there first-ever postseason game to the Philadelphia Eagles by a score of 21-0.

When the 1950's rolled around along came head coach John Michelosen, coaching from 1948 to 1951 compiling a record for those years with a mark of 20-26-2. In 1952 coach Joe Bach took over at the helm for the second time; he first coached the team for the '35 and '36 seasons. The Steelers became the last team to let go of the single wing for the T-formation in 1952. After the '54 season Bach resigned for health reasons, being replaced by then assistant coach Walt Kiesling who actually coached three different times; '39-40, '41-44 and finally, '54-56.

With the decade of the 60's in sight, Buddy Parker was named head coach in 1957 and over the next eight seasons he led the Steelers to five non-losing seasons along with Hall of Fame quarterback Bobby Layne. In 1962, Parker and Layne led the team to a 9-5 record which landed them in a playoff game against Detroit. The Steelers lost the game by a mark of 17-10. Parker rounded out his Steelers years with a record of

51-48-6 which rankes third among all-time Steelers coaches for career wins.

In the year 1964 the Steelers made team history by retiring jersey No. 70 which belonged to former defensive tackle Ernie Stautner. Stautner, a 1969 hall of famer, remains the only Steelers player to have a jersey retired.

Short head coaching stints by Mike Nixon in '65 and Bill Austin from '66-68 were followed by the hiring of head coach Chuck Noll in January, 1969. The rebuilding process began with Noll by his first draft choice being none other than Hall of Famer and defensive great, Joe Green.

A skinny 1-13 record in the '69 season gave Noll the first choice in 1970 when Noll smartly grabbed up a quarterback named Terry Bradshaw, another Hall of Famer. The third round brought yet another Hall of Famer to Noll named Mel Blount, a soon-to-be blistering cornerback. Jack Ham was added to the stable of players in 1971 and the team made room for Franco Harris in the '72 draft. In total, Noll gathered nine players who are in the Hall of Fame via the draft.

The year 1970 saw the opening of Three Rivers Stadium, giving them a permanent home rather than playing at Forbes Field and Pitt Stadium. A gradual improvement in the early '70's resulted in an impressive 11-3 record in '72. In the first playoff game played in Three Rivers saw the Steelers beat the Oakland Raiders by the score of 13-7 with the "Immaculate Reception" in the final minute of the game by Franco Harris. Even though the Steelers lost the following game to the Dolphins, the Steelers reached a pinnacle point in the NFL.

While it took 40 years for the Steelers to get their first division title, the Steelers saw unprecedented success in the decade of the '70's. In 1973, the Steelers won a wild card berth with a record of 10-4 but the Raiders paid the Steelers back by beating them 33-14 in the playoffs.

1974 proved to be magical by winning Super Bowl IX against the Minnesota Vikings by a score of 16-6 and Mr. Art Rooney was finally handed his first Lombardi trophy. The 1975 season saw the Steelers win 11 straight games to finish 12-2 and claim their second consecutive division crown. After defeating Baltimore and the Raiders in the playoffs the Steelers became the third team in history, along with

Green Bay and Miami, to win back-to-back Super Bowls with a 21-17 win in Super Bowl X against the Cowboys.

The bicentennial year was a struggle early on for the Steelers via a 1-4 start before winning nine straight including five shutouts to win the division with a mark of 10-4. The Steelers defeated Baltimore in the playoffs but got beat by Oakland, after both Rocky Bleier and Franco Harris came up injured. The following year, 1977 were beaten by the Broncos by 12 points in the first round of the playoffs after posting a 9-5 regular season mark.

1978 was a strong year for the Steelers to say the least. After a league best of 14-2 regular season mark and playoff wins against Denver and Houston, the Steelers defeated their rival in the Cowboys of Dallas, Texas in a close game with a score of 35-31, making the Steelers the first three time Super Bowl winning team.

As if all that was not enough for the decade of the '70's, the Steelers set another record by being the first team in the League to win four Super Bowls, beating the Rams of Los Angeles by a score of 31-19. Super Bowl XIV was not only the fourth Super Bowl win for the Steelers but also the second time the Steelers won back to back Super Bowls. It is no wonder why the Steelers were tagged the "team of the decade" for the 70's with a hefty six consecutive AFC crowns, eight straight playoff appearances and four Super Bowl wins.

The new decade of the '80's watched the Steelers struggle, not able to make the playoffs in 1980 or 1981. However, in 1982 the Steelers celebrated 50 years in the league and made the playoffs with a record of 6-3 with a season that was interrupted by a strike. A fifty year anniversary celebration was held, a week of activities with thousands of fans attracted to Pittsburgh for the big celebration. The anniversary season ended with a playoff loss to San Diego. Three Rivers went on a 10 year dry run concerning playoff games; the next playoff game for Three Rivers would not come until the 1992 season.

The '83 regular season, the Steelers won their eighth division title with a record of 10-6 but fell in the playoffs to the Los Angeles Raiders. The following year the Steelers won their ninth division title and advanced to the AFC Championship game with a win at Denver. A 45-28 pounding by Miami in the AFC Championship game held the Steelers from a fifth Steelers Super Bowl appearance.

The Steelers saw 13 consecutive non-losing seasons come to an end in 1985 with a finish of 7-8 and a 6-10 finish in 1986. Playoff hopes lasted quite a while in the '87 season until the Steelers lost two games at the end of the season to finish up 8-7 during a season shortened by a strike.

In 1988, the Steelers suffered with a mark of 5-11 on the season; the worst in 19 years. The next season was not much different with losses with marks of 51-0 and 41-0 in the first two games with the offense failing to score in the first month of the season. The young team fought back and ended up with a record of 9-7 and getting a wild card berth on the final weekend of the season. A nail-biting 26-23 overtime playoff win in Houston was followed by a heartbreaking loss by the score of 24-23 to the Broncos in a divisional playoff game.

The year 1990 saw a 9-7 finish and left the Steelers in a three-way tie for the AFC Central lead but the Steelers were ousted from playoff contention via a 2-4 division record. The next years team finished second in the division despite a record of 7-9, winning the last games that Noll coached against the Bengals and the Browns.

The Day after Christmas, 1991, Chuck Noll announced his retirement from the league after a long and successful 39 season career with the last 23 of those years being spent with the Steelers of Pittsburgh. Noll left as the fifth-winningest coach in the history of the NFL and the only coach to win four Super Bowls. In 1993, Nolls' first year of eligibility, he was elected to the Hall of Fame.

1992 saw the arrival of Bill Cowher, the youngest coach in the league at the time; 34 years old. In coach Cowhers' first season the Steelers took the AFC Central division crown for the first time since 1984 with a mark of 11-5. Coach Cowher was honored with eh Associated Press Coach of the Year and six Steelers played in the Pro Bowl, the most in more than ten years.

Under Cowher the Steelers became the first AFC team since the merger in 1970 to win its 10th division title. The Steelers had home field advantage throughout the playoffs; however, in the first playoff game in Three Rivers in 10 years saw a Steelers loss to Buffalo by a score of 24-3.

The '93 season afforded the Steelers a wild card berth which was the first time since the 1983-1984 that the Steelers had back to back playoff contenders. The Steelers lost to Kansas City in the wild card game, 27-24 in overtime.

In the 1994 campaign, the team won seven of the final regular eight games for the strongest finish since 1978, capturing their second division title in three years with the best record in the AFC; 12-4. The Steelers defeated the Cleveland Browns in the first round of the playoffs which afforded the team to host its first AFC playoff game since 1979. A down-to-the-wire game ensued against the San Diego Chargers with the Chargers winning the game by a score of 17-13.

At the young age of 38, Bill Cowher became the youngest head coach to lead his team to a Super Bowl. Along the way, the team grabbed its third AFC Central division title in four years, made their fourth playoff appearance in a row and won their first AFC title game since 1979. The Steelers took care of business against the Bills and the Colts after a first round bye and beat the two teams 40-21 and 20-16 respectively. The Steelers met the Cowboys in Super Bowl XXX and met defeat as well as they went down to the Cowboys by a mark of 27-17.

In 1996, Cowher was forced to use 40 starters because of injuries over the course of the season. The Steelers' strong and upbeat attitude led to a 10-6 season finish and their fifth trip in a row to the playoffs. Cowher garnered his 50th career regular-season win in 73 starts making him the eighth fastest coach to reach such a plateau. He finished the season with 57 wins slotting him just behind his predecessor, coach Noll as the second winningest coach in team history.

In 1997, the Steelers grabbed their fourth consecutive AFC Central title, posting an 11-5 mark. They lost to Denver in the title game and were one play away from their sixth Super Bowl appearance; they lost the game by a score of 24-21.

The team finished a meager 7-9 in 1998, losing their last five regular-season games and missing the playoffs for the first time under head coach Cowher. This year was also the first time in Cowhers' 14 years of coaching that he was associated with a team with a losing record.

1999 was a losing season as well with a 6-10 record including a six-game losing streak. The fourth place AFC Central division finish was the teams worst under Cowher.

In the new century; the decade of the 2000's saw a renewal of the Steelers commitment. The Steelers started the 2000 season with losing its first three games but rebounded to finished up 9-7 and just missed a postseason appearance. The most memorable thing in the year of 2000 was perhaps it being the final season for Three Rivers Stadium. The Steelers had victories in four of their final sox home games at the old Stadium. The Steelers won the final game, 23 against the Redskins on December 16th with over 58,000 fans on hand which was a record for the season.

The Steelers began a new era at Heinz Field in 2003 with a stellar 13-3 regular season record which was the best in the AFC which afforded the Steelers an AFC Champion Game.

The opening game at Heinz was set for September 16 but the terrorist attacks cancelled all games that weekend which caused the inaugural game to be held on October 7th with a 16-7 win against the Bengals.

The Steelers beat the defending Super Bowl Champion Ravens, 27-10 in the AFC Divisional Playoffs in the first-ever postseason game at the new home of the Steelers. The team then lost in the AFC Championship game against the Patriots who ended up being the Super Bowl champs that year.

The Steelers entered the 2002 season with high hopes and Super Bowl aspirations but those hopes disappeared with a road loss to the Titans. The 2003 season was a struggle with an eventual 6-10 mark on the season and out of the playoffs for the first time in three years.

The Steelers bounced back in a big way in 2004, becoming the first AFC team to win 15 games in the regular season and ended with a bright 15-1 record. They ended up losing the AFC Championship Game to the pesky Patriots by a score of 41-27. The season had another bright spot; nine players selected to play in the Pro Bowl game which was the most since the 1979 season.

The first 12 games of the 2005 season saw Pittsburgh sitting at 7-5 but the team rallied to win its next four and get a sixth seed in the playoffs. The Steelers went on to win an unprecedented three road games in the playoffs to get a Super Bowl Berth in Super Bowl XL in Detroit vs. the Seahawks. The Steelers won their fifth Super Bowl by a 21-10 finish over the Seahawks. The ever-solid Hines Ward was the MVP of the game and also pulled in the 43 yard pass by Antwaan Randle El on a trick play in the middle of the fourth quarter to seal the deal.

2006 saw the Cowher era come to a halt with the coach resigning with an 8-8 mark on the season. Bill Cowher left with a second-best in team history 166-99-1. The coaching vacancy was filled with Mike Tomlin, a 34 year old coach which was the youngest head coach in the NFL at the time. Tomlin was hired on January 22, 2007. Tomlin became the second first-season coach in team history to make the playoffs as he and his team finished 10-6 and was the AFC North division winners.

Coach Mike Tomlin won division titles in his first two seasons which was the first coach to do so in team history. The Steelers finished 12-4 and capturing the AFC North division title for the second consecutive year. The Steelers and Tomlin went on to defeat the Chargers and the Ravens to gain a berth in Super Bowl XLIII in Tampa, Florida versus the Cardinals. The big game saw the Steelers as the first team in the NFL to capture six Super Bowl titles when they beat the Cardinals, 27-23. With the win, Tomlin became the youngest head coach to ever win a Super Bowl in the History of the NFL. With just 35 seconds remaining in the game, Rothlisberger threw a pass for a touchdown to Santonio Holmes to seal the win. Holmes was the MVP of the game.

1974 Pittsburgh Steelers Roster

Head Coach: *Chuck Noll

- To be listed, a player must have played at least one game for the team during this season.
- Hall of Fame
- Primary starter

DB	Jimmy Allen	DB	Glen Edwards
RB	Rocky Bleier	RB	John Fuqua
CB	* Mel Blount	DE/DT	Steve Furness
LB	Ed Bradley	WR	Reggie Garrett
QB	* Terry Bradshaw	K	Roy Gerela
T/TE	Larry Brown	QB	Joe Gilliam
C/G	Jim Clack	T	Gordon Gravelle
DB	Dick Conn	DT	* Joe Greene
DT/NT	Charlie Davis	DE	L. C. Greenwood
G	Sam Davis	TE	Randy Grossman
RB	Steve Davis	LB	* Jack Ham
T/G	Rich Druschel	QB	Terry Hanratty

RB	* Franco Harris
RB	Reggie Harrison
DT	Ernie Holmes
LB	Marv Kellum
T/C	Jon Kolb
LB	* Jack Lambert
WR	Frank Lewis
C/DT	Ray Mansfield
TE	John McMakin
G/T	Gerry Mullins
RB/DB	Preston Pearson
T/G	Dave Reavis
LB	Andy Russell
WR	Ron Shanklin
DB	Donnie Shell
WR	* John Stallworth
WR	* Lynn Swann
DB	J. T. Thomas
LB	Loren Toews
DB	Mike Wagner
P	Bobby Walden
C/G	* Mike Webster
ADE	Dwight White
DE	Jim Wolf

About the Author

Peter Cannizzaro is a 43 year old Agriculture teacher from a small rural town in Southeast Louisiana; Folsom is a village of only several thousand people one hour North of New Orleans, Louisiana. Peter is married to the former Holly Jones, has three beautiful children; two daughters; Nicolai, age 14, Scout, age 9 and a son; Cross, age 6.

Peter has a B.S. in Animal Science/Pre-veterinary Medicine from Southeastern Louisiana University at Hammond, LA. M.S. in Vocational Education from Louisiana State University along with a Ph.D. in Human Resource Education and Workforce Development from Louisiana State University

Dr. Cannizzaro has worked in the field of education for the last 18 years while also being a professional public address announcer, auctioneer and has just kicked off a career in voice over work. Additionally, Dr. Cannizzaro motivationally speaks to adults and youth across the country on subjects ranging from leadership to teamwork to conflict resolution.

To inquire about any of Dr. Cannizzaro's speaking work, fees, and booking dates, please contact him at <u>petercannizzaro@charter.net</u>

REFERENCES

Roster information retrieved on 6.1.10 from:
http://www.jt-sw.com/football/pro/rosters.nsf/Annual/1974-pit

Steelers History information retrieved on 6.1.10 from: http://prod.www.
steelers.clubs.nfl.com/
history/tradition-of-excellence.html